Dee Dee

Written by Betty Haggard

Illustrated by Jess Jung

ISBN: 0692981780
ISBN 13: 9780692981788

I dedicate this book to
my four Great Grandchildren,
Dominic, Ana, William, and Kaylee.

May they always live the
Golden Rule.

I'm grateful for the encouragement of my daughter Jeri and my son Terry to bring my Dee Dee stories to publication and to the following contributers:

Carolyn Willis for editing.

Susan Page for finding the illustrator.

Jan Madison for the photograph of me.

Jessica Jung, who so beautifully illustrated and formatted this book.

I am the cutest puppy
in the whole world.

Grandma Freddye said so.
She had many other puppies live
with her so I know it must be true.

She named me Dee Dee
which is short for, Darling Dog.
Sometimes she calls me Girl.

I grew up pretty fast.
I never got very tall.
My legs are short, but I can run fast.

My hair is dark grey.
My eyes are dark too.
  At the end of my tail
   there are
   three white hairs.

I'm a Cairn Terrier.

My food and water bowls are pink.
Pink is Grandma Freddye's
favorite color.

I have a pink leash
and a pink collar with sparkles.
Even my sweater is pink.

Pink is a happy color

and I like it too.

There is a pet door leading to the back yard.
It is a wonderful place to play.
There is grass, trees and
pots of flowers.
The fence is high enough
to keep me safe.

Grandma has a big swing with
soft cushions.
She sits there on warm sunny days
and I sleep with my
head on her lap.

I'm learning when she says,

"shh-h-h or no,"

I don't jump
on people, or bark
for too long.

She tells me I'm a good girl
and pets me when I do
what she says.
Sometimes I get a treat.

When I go to the groomer,
it takes a long time.
I have to stay in a kennel while I wait my turn.

My groomer's name is Cindy. She is
kind and tells me how glad she is to see me.
She even has shampoo that
doesn't sting my eyes.
Cindy cuts my hair and I hold still while
she trims around my eyes. After she cleans my
ears, she washes me all over. Next, I get brushed
while Cindy uses a hair dryer to dry my hair.
Sometimes, she cuts my toenails and it doesn't
hurt at all.

When she is finished,
she sprays me with something
that smells good and puts a pink bow
on top of my head.
Grandma Freddye comes to get me.
She asks me all about my day.
I try to tell her with short growls and
soft barks.
She hugs me and tells me how pretty I am
and how good I smell. I had a good time with
Cindy, but I'm happy Grandma
is taking me home.

On our way home, we stop at the car wash.
I have never been before.
Two men use a big brush to wash the
wheels, mirrors and windows. The car is pulled
into a dark room with big brushes rolling all over us.
Soap is everywhere.
Water is spraying the soap away.
I am afraid.
I hear loud blowing sounds.
Big rags are wiping
the water off the car.

I am so scared that I get down
on the floor of the car by Grandma's feet.

She tells me everything is alright
and pets me, but I'm still afraid.
Finally, we drive out of there.

Two men dry the car with towels.

Now we are going home.
I'm glad because I've had enough adventure
for one day.
I think I will take a nap.

Betty Haggard
has travelled the world.
She has written many
short stories including
the "Dee Dee" series of
children's books.
Betty lives in
Washington State.

Jess Jung is an illustrator who
collaborated with the author to
create these beautiful illustrations.
Jess spends her time painting
custom pet portraits.
She can be reached at
jessjungartist@gmail.com

Look for
Dee Dee's Christmas!

Made in the USA
San Bernardino, CA
02 May 2019